A Fast Walk
Through a
Long History

ALSO BY HORACE RANDALL WILLIAMS

The Ku Klux Klan: A Legacy of Hate (ED., 1982)

Montgomery Quizine (WITH GEORGE LITTLETON, 1988)

*Hard Labor: A Report on Day Labor Pools and
Temporary Employment* (ED., 1988)

*When Hate Groups Come to Town: A Handbook of Effective
Community Responses* (ED., 1992)

Johnnie: The Life of Johnnie Rebecca Carr (1995)

*The Children Coming On: A Retrospective
of the Montgomery Bus Boycott* (ED., 1996)

W. E. B. Du Bois: A Scholar's Courageous Life (2001)

This Day in Civil Rights History (WITH BEN BEARD, 2004)

*Weren't No Good Times:
Personal Accounts of Slavery in Alabama* (ED., 2005)

*No Man's Yoke on My Shoulders:
Personal Accounts of Slavery in Florida* (ED., 2006)

*The Alabama Guide:
Our People, Resources, and Government* (ED., 2009)

*Sports Rehabilitation and the Human Spirit: How the Landmark
Program at the Lakeshore Foundation Rebuilds Bodies
and Restores Lives* (WITH ANITA SMITH, 2013)

*History Refused to Die: The Enduring Legacy of African American
Art in Alabama* (CONTRIBUTOR, 2015)

100 Things You Need To Know About Alabama (2016)

A FAST WALK THROUGH A LONG HISTORY

A Summary of the American Civil Rights Struggle from 1619 in Jamestown to 1965 in Selma

HORACE RANDALL WILLIAMS

NEWSOUTH BOOKS

Montgomery

NewSouth Books
105 S. Court Street
Montgomery, AL 36104

Cataloging-in-Publication Data
978-1-60306-434-6 (trade paper)
978-1-60306-435-4 (ebook)

A version of this essay first appeared in *History Refused to Die: The
Enduring Legacy of African American Art in Alabama* (Tinwood
Books, 2015). It was also the basis of a lecture by the author on
April 23, 2015, at the Montgomery Museum of Fine Arts coinciding
with an exhibit of works by fourteen African American artists from
Alabama. Special thanks to Suzanne La Rosa, who helped me with the
research and images, and to historian Mills Thornton, who made key
suggestions and straightened me out on several points I had muddled.

Printed in the United States of America

Contents

I.

Slavery / 7

II.

Civil War / 12

III.

Reconstruction and Redemption / 16

IV.

The Jim Crow Era / 19

V.

The Modern Civil Rights Movement / 22

I.

Slavery

We often hear that the civil rights movement began with the Montgomery Bus Boycott in 1955, gathered focus in Little Rock (1957) and Greensboro (1960) and during the Freedom Rides (1961), reached crises in Birmingham (1963) and Mississippi's Freedom Summer (1964), and came to a great confrontation in Selma (1965). That historical shorthand is not false, but it is not the big picture.

The larger truth is that the foundation of the modern American civil rights movement was laid in Jamestown, Virginia. When the first African slaves to arrive in the American colonies stepped off a Dutch ship there in 1619, it became historically inevitable that civil rights activists would step onto Selma's Edmund Pettus Bridge in 1965.

Inevitable may be too strong a word. *Events were set in motion.* Counterfactual history might argue that American slavery could have turned out differently, and without slavery, of course, there would have been no Jim Crow segregation and thus no need for a civil rights movement.

Alas, greed, ignorance, religion, technology, and inhumanity are powerful forces; when they collide, bad things happen.

Those first African Americans—literally—were technically not slaves. They had been part of the plunder from a Spanish slave ship captured by Dutch traders, and they were brought to Virginia to help meet the English colonists' rising need for labor, chiefly in agriculture. These Africans joined the many white indentured servants already at work in the colonies.

However, indentured servants eventually earned their freedom, and as the inflow of white European indentured servants slowed during the seventeenth century, merchants and landowners in the colonies began to rationalize a shift in attitude toward their dark-skinned workers. Slavery itself was ancient, but it was historically not race-based and it was not permanent. The early African slave trade was justified by European religious belief that Africans were heathens and their captivity was God's will. Slave traders and owners also cited the Genesis story of God cursing the dark-skinned Ham. Either way, blacks were *other* and could be treated differently than whites. In the British colonies of North America, the attitudinal shift involved culture, religion, and law, but its roots were in economic exploitation and white privilege. Between 1640 and 1705, indentured servitude for blacks gradually evolved into slavery, and slavery spread throughout the colonies.

Still, the growth of slavery was slow except in the colonies which had developed labor-intensive plantation agriculture, notably Virginia, Maryland, and the Carolinas. In 1680, slaves were not quite 10 percent of the Southern population but by 1790 were a third. By 1750, New York, for example, had 65,682 whites and 11,014 blacks (free and enslaved), while Virginia had 129,581 whites and 101,452 blacks (mostly enslaved). But by 1790, the respective totals in New York were 314,366 whites and 21,193 slaves, but 442,117 whites and 292,627 slaves in Virginia (42 percent of the slaves in the U.S. at that time).

After the American Revolution, for a nation that had willed itself into existence based on the principle "that all men are created equal," slavery was a divisive issue. The 1781 Articles of Confederation were mute on slavery, leaving the matter to the individual states. Delegates to the 1787 Constitutional Convention split over the issue of representation by population in the House of Representatives. Southern states wanted to include slaves in the population figures, thus increasing their power; northern states with fewer slaves did not. The delegates compromised by counting each slave as three-fifths of a person. Another compromise was that the import of new slaves from Africa—already banned in ten states—could not be ended by Congress until 1808. A final compromise was inclusion of a fugitive slave clause sought by the slave states in return for concessions to the North on shipping and trade.

These compromises had far-reaching consequences, including the kidnapping of blacks in the North and forcing them into slavery in the South, the domination of the Electoral College by the South, and the import of so many additional new African slaves that it facilitated the expansion of slavery into new U.S. territories.

Northern delegates may have agreed to these compromises in part because the general trends were toward industrialization and the abolition of slavery. However, in the early 1790s, the cotton gin was invented, making the separation of cotton fiber from cotton seed exponentially more efficient. Cotton was mostly grown in the favorable climate and soils of the southern U.S., where most slaves already were. Suddenly the product of slaves' labor became vastly more valuable to slave owners. Northern and British textile plants could absorb all the cotton the South could export, so slave owners sought larger and larger plantations and more and more slaves to do the work of cotton cultivation and harvesting.

Around the time of the development of the cotton gin, Alabama was a part of the Old Southwest—frontier territory, mostly occupied by Indian tribes and partly held by Spain. In 1798, what is now Mississippi and Alabama became the Mississippi Territory, which was expanded several times, until in 1817 Mississippi became a state, followed by Alabama in 1819.

The rush for the rich, fertile lands in the two new states began immediately. First the area had to be stolen from the native Indian populations. Andrew Jackson had already defeated the Creeks in 1814, and ensuing treaties gradually opened up more Creek, Choctaw, and Chickasaw lands for white settlement. "Alabama Fever" quickly infected planters, especially from the Carolinas and Georgia, who moved their entire plantation operations, including their slaves, into the area, predominantly in the central Black Belt area of the state and the Tennessee River valley of the northern part.

Thus came the era of King Cotton. In 1830, some 750,000 bales of cotton were produced in the U.S.; by 1850, the crop had grown to 2.85 million bales. In 1790, there were 654,000 slaves in the southern states; by 1830 there were almost two million, and by the eve of the Civil War, almost four million. As we know, the descendants of these slaves from 1860 made the civil rights movement a century later.

For the forty years of the antebellum period, 1820–60, Alabama boomed as King Cotton made many white men extremely rich. Wealth was made off both the labor of slaves and the buying and selling of slaves. The slave population continued to increase during this period, from importation of slaves and from births to slave mothers already in the state. By 1860, Alabama's population of about one million was 53 percent white, 44 percent slave, and a few percent other, including a few thousand free blacks.

Given the steady growth in their profits, slave owners during this period understandably believed, on the one hand, that this prosperity could continue indefinitely, and, on the other hand, that they were justified in doing anything necessary to preserve it. In 1805, the one million U.S. slaves were worth an estimated $300 million. By 1860, the four million slaves were valued at about $3 billion (about $75 billion today), or roughly equal to the total value of all the agricultural buildings and lands in the South. Slaves contributed more than half the labor in the South.

As slave labor became more essential and slave value increased, Southern whites intensified their political, legal, and cultural control over the institution. Attitudes toward slaves hardened even further and brutal punishments became more common. Not merely the condition of bondage but even the essential humanity of men became defined by skin color or race. John C. Calhoun of South Carolina, regarded as the greatest Southern politician of the era, declared slavery a social good and a benefit to Africans:

> Never before has the black race . . . from the dawn of history to the present day, attained a condition so civilized and so improved, not only physically, but morally and intellectually. It came to us in a low, degraded, and savage condition, and in the course of a few generations it has grown up under the fostering care of our institutions.

Then the U.S. Supreme Court's *Dred Scott v. Sandford* decision of 1857 established as law that no person with African blood could be an American citizen and that the federal government had no power to regulate slavery in newly acquired federal territories. The stage was set for even greater conflict.

II.

Civil War

Let's get this out of the way up front: The Civil War was fought over slavery.

Secession followed a national dispute over the future of slavery, specifically whether slavery would be allowed in new U.S. territories acquired in the Mexican War of 1846–48. Abolitionists wanted slavery to be illegal in these territories, while slavery supporters knew that barring slavery in any states made from the new territories would upset the balance of power in the Congress and probably lead to a national abolition of slavery. Most white Southerners then cited, and many still do, states' rights as the major issue of the war, but the states' right at issue was the right to continue to own slaves. The North had turned against this right, while the South upheld it. People who argue otherwise today are either ignorant or are willfully distorting the history. Even a cursory glance at the record reveals that slavery was the main issue.

Lincoln was a declared opponent of the expansion of slavery; his election in 1860 fueled secessionist sentiment. Seven states seceded before Lincoln was inaugurated, and Jefferson Davis, former U.S. secretary of war and U.S. senator from Mississippi, was chosen as president of the new Confederacy. Davis's view of slavery was clear:

> [Slavery] was established by decree of Almighty God . . . it
> is sanctioned in the Bible, in both Testaments, from Genesis to
> Revelation . . . it has existed in all ages, has been found among

the people of the highest civilization, and in nations of the highest proficiency in the arts.

Davis's vice president, former Georgia Congressman Alexander Stephens, declared that the Confederacy's

. . . foundations are laid, its corner-stone rests, upon the great truth that the negro is not equal to the white man; that slavery—subordination to the superior race—is his natural and normal condition.

Four horrific years of war later, the Confederates' surrender ended the conflict, the Union was preserved, and white and black Southerners faced the challenge of living together in a new order. Living together was key, for although the former African American slaves were now freedmen, they mostly stayed in the South. Thousands had escaped to the North during the war—some 200,000 blacks served in the Union military—and remained there afterwards, but the great majority never left the areas where they had been enslaved. As early as 1820, there had been efforts to repatriate ex-slaves to Africa, and these efforts continued on a small scale, especially to Liberia, but ultimately had modest impact.

The 1863 Emancipation Proclamation had symbolic effect but in actuality freed few slaves and left their legal status unclear. In January 1865 Congress adopted the 13th Amendment, ending the legal "three-fifths of a person" recognition of slavery, and when the amendment was ratified in December 1865, millions of ex-slaves became freedmen. However, most had no resources, education, homes, jobs, or preparation for independent living. Their former masters had land but no workers, and few had much money, having lost all their slave capital, whatever they had put into Confederate currency or bonds, and whatever losses they had incurred due to the war itself. An estimated 22.6 percent of white Southern males between the ages of 20 and 24 died as a result of combat or illness during the war. And many soldiers who survived were maimed for life; in the year after the war, Mississippi spent a fifth of its state revenues providing artificial arms and legs to war veterans.

The war had been fought mostly in the South, and the desolation was almost unimaginable. A visitor to Charleston wrote, "A city of ruins, desolation, and vacant houses, of rotting wharves, deserted warehouses, and grass-grown streets. That is Charleston. The beauty and pride of the city are dead." Things were no better in the rural areas, where most of the ex-slaves were. Wrote one Virginian: "We had no cattle, hogs, sheep, or horses, or anything else. The barns were all burned, chimneys standing without houses and houses standing without roofs, or doors, or windows." As Margaret Mitchell would famously write, all was "gone with the wind."

White and black Southerners were living together in their post-war misery and poverty. The ex-slaves had their freedom and their hope for a better future, though the latter was often elusive. Millie Freeman wrote: "It seemed like it took a long time for freedom to come. Everything just kept on like it was. We heard that lots of slaves was getting land and some mules to set up for theirselves. I never knowed any what got land or mules nor nothing."

If Lincoln had lived, things might have turned out differently. General William T. Sherman described a visit with Lincoln in the White House:

> I inquired of the President if he was all ready for the end of the war. He said he was all ready; all he wanted of us was to defeat the opposing armies, and to get the men composing the Confederate armies back to their homes, at work on their farms, and in their shops. I was more than ever impressed by his kindly nature and his deep and earnest sympathy with the afflictions of

the whole people. His earnest desire seemed to [be to] end the war speedily, and to restore the men of both sections to their homes. He had made it clear that he wanted to save the Union, then heal it, to return farmers to their fields and merchants to their stores, in both South and North, to restore families, to give the freedmen a helping hand toward independent life.

But Lincoln did not live, and the post-war reconciliation he had spoken of in his second inaugural address—"With malice toward none, with charity for all . . . let us strive on to finish the work we are in, to bind up the nation's wounds"—did not come to pass under his successor, Vice President Andrew Johnson. Nor were the nation's wounds bound up, in part because Southern whites possessed one thing after the war that their freedmen brothers in misery lacked: a seemingly bottomless well of bitterness and resentment that would fester for decades to come.

III.

Reconstruction and Redemption

The Confederates had lost the war, but they immediately set out to win the peace. One of their first goals was to reestablish social control over the four million freedmen. As slaves, they had been property, with no legal rights. A variety of Slave Codes had regulated slave behavior and especially movement, in hopes of minimizing runaways and uprisings. The 13th Amendment knocked down the slave codes, but in 1865 and 1866 most of the former slave states enacted a series of Black Codes that were similar to the Slave Codes.

The Black Codes were also intended to restore the cheap labor that had been lost with emancipation of the slaves. All freedmen were required to have a job. Those who could not prove they had a job or a permanent residence could be arrested for vagrancy and fined. If they could not pay the fine, they could be bound out to a term of labor supervised by whites—sometimes their former owners. Violators of the Black Codes were subject to harsh punishments such as branding or whipping.

No wonder that many blacks and Northern whites questioned whether slavery had actually ended. This contributed to widespread political discontent with President Johnson's administration and to the takeover by Radical Republicans in the congressional elections of 1866. Republican governments, backed by occupying federal troops, were then set up in all the former Confederate states except Virginia. The Freedmen's Bureau expanded its activities, the black codes were repealed, more rights were granted to blacks, and political rights of ex-Confederates were restricted. The Civil Rights Acts of 1866 and 1875 and the 1868 ratification of the 14th Amendment, which overrode *Dred Scott*, further established African American equality under the law.

Reconstruction was a hopeful time for Alabama's African Americans. They voted, held political office, and saw new educational, vocational, and civic opportunities, though not without resentment, resistance, and violence. The first incarnation of the Ku Klux Klan arose during this time, and the hooded nightriders were merely among various guerrilla and terrorist tactics that ex-Confederates used against blacks, their white Republican allies, and the occupying federal troops. Ultimately, Reconstruction was defeated, and the nation's promise to the freed slaves turned out to be, to paraphrase Martin Luther King Jr. a century later, a check that bounced. "Redemption" followed, as ex-Confederate white Democrats took back control of state and local governments in the South and the economy from the coalition of white and black Republicans that had governed in the decade following the war. In 1873, the Slaughterhouse Cases emanating from New Orleans gutted the 14th Amendment and left most citizens' rights in the control of the individual states. Opponents of Radical Reconstruction charged that it had been grotesquely corrupt; contemporary historians mostly agree that the period was rife with corruption on the parts of both Democrats and Republicans and that the coalition of blacks, carpetbaggers, and scalawags were no more corrupt than those who replaced them.

In any case, by 1877, Reconstruction was done; the freedmen were on their own. In 1883 the Supreme Court overturned the Civil Rights Act of 1875, which had barred discrimination in inns, theaters, and other public places, and ruled that the 14th Amendment did not forbid private discrimination. For the remainder of the 19th century, African Americans saw their civil rights steadily diminished and their economic opportunities narrowed as more and more restrictive conditions were imposed on them through sharecropping, convict labor, and outright violence. Convict leasing—"slavery by another name"—was particularly egregious. The revenues to Southern states from the leasing of convicts to private employers provided additional incentive to arrest blacks for little or no reason. Once leased, the convicts were often poorly fed, clothed, and housed, and labored in extreme and dangerous conditions. Many died. In Tennessee, the proportion of African Americans in the prison system increased from 33 percent in 1865 to 67 percent between 1877 and 1879. Alabama did not end convict leasing until 1928.

The Panic of 1893 led to a brief moment of optimism as blacks and poor whites made common cause under the banner of populism, but ultimately racism and white supremacy prevailed, and the close of the 19th and the opening of the 20th century brought almost total disenfranchisement, a new wave of lynchings and other terror, and a newly intensified system of statutory discrimination.

IV.

The Jim Crow Era

This harsh system of segregation—akin to apartheid in South Africa—permeated every aspect of life in the southern United States throughout the first half of the 20th century. Segregation could be found in the north as well, though by custom rather than by statute. But rising against segregation were gradual steps in the courts, in national policy, and in organizations within the black community and churches, and in a few interracial organizations.

The charismatic Marcus Garvey attempted to establish black nationalism and repatriation to Africa, but his movement never gained traction. Black political strategy coalesced under the competing leadership of Booker T. Washington and W. E. B. Du Bois. Washington, the great educator at Tuskegee Institute, privately supported the building of black institutions but publicly argued that accommodation to segregation was the best African Americans could hope for, and that they should strive for fair treatment under the law but in other respects remain culturally and socially separate from whites. The intellectual Du Bois argued that blacks should demand full integration and force the U.S. to live up to the principles of equality trumpeted by its founding documents. In fairness to Washington, Du Bois's views were easier to promote in the North, while Washington had to deal with the brutal realities of sharecropper poverty, vigilante violence, and almost total white supremacy in Alabama and the other Deep South states.

In Alabama, the vast majority of blacks had been disenfranchised by the 1901 Constitution; from 1904 to 1966, Alabama electoral ballots bore the slogan "White Supremacy for the Right" under the Democratic Party symbol.

Nationally, the NAACP was organized in 1909 and chapters were established even in the segregated South. In Atlanta, the Commission on Interracial Cooperation (the South's first integrated advocacy group, later known as the Southern Regional Council) organized in 1919. The Communist Party, among others, organized radical activists across racial lines and gained converts following the Scottsboro Boys case in 1931. The Southern Tenant Farmers' Union united poor white and black sharecroppers in the 1930s. In 1938, the Southern Conference for Human Welfare brought blacks and whites together (even though city officials enforced segregated seating) at a meeting in Birmingham attended by First Lady Eleanor Roosevelt.

Franklin D. Roosevelt's New Deal agencies brought some relief and employment to poor blacks during the Great Depression, thus instigating the transition of black political allegiance from the party of Lincoln to the Democratic Party. On a small scale, blacks began registering to vote and forming local political organizations, often affiliated with the NAACP, to press for better treatment, more schools, housing, and so on. Beginning in the 1930s, NAACP attorneys Charles Hamilton Houston and Thurgood Marshall conceived a brick-by-brick legal strategy that by the 1950s would lead to victory over school segregation as a matter of law if not in fact. Meanwhile, the Julius Rosenwald Fund built more than 5,000 black schools across the South between 1917 and 1948 to counter gross disparities in Southern states' education funding for whites and blacks. It had been illegal in most Southern states to teach slaves to read and write, and literacy rates and educational opportunities for African Americans remained shockingly low until the mid twentieth century.

Blacks had gone to war for the U.S. during the Civil War, the 19th-century Indian wars in the West, the Spanish–American War of 1898, and during World War I, though usually in menial support jobs. But the entry of the U.S. into World War II brought a push for blacks to be allowed to serve in all military roles. The Tuskegee Airmen famously disproved the racist view that blacks could not pilot aircraft in combat, and the lesser-known Montford Point Marines and the all-black 92nd Infantry Division proved that blacks were as capable soldiers as whites—and as willing to fight and die for their country. The performance of black servicemen was a rebuke to white supremacists, and in 1948 President Truman used an executive order to desegregate the U.S. armed forces.

Following WWII, black veterans became leaders in the emerging civil rights and voting rights movements, asking poignantly why they should have fought to rid Europe of Hitler's oppression when they still confronted legalized racism in their own homeland. Some whites were beginning to listen, significantly some federal judges.

In 1944, the courts struck down the all-white primary election scheme in Texas. In a series of cases in 1938, 1948, and 1950, NAACP lawyers won court rulings against segregation in law schools, and in 1954, the U.S. Supreme Court ruled—in a consolidated case brought by the NAACP—that segregated education generally was unconstitutional, thus overturning the separate but equal doctrine that had governed U.S. law since the *Plessy v. Ferguson* ruling of 1896. The *Brown v. Board of Education* findings against segregation itself—not merely the gross inequities in school access and funding—changed everything and set the stage for act five in the continuing African American struggle to overcome the legacy of slavery.

V.

The Modern Civil Rights Movement

What happened in Montgomery in 1955 is now more or less acknowledged as the start of the 20th-century movement that finally put an end to legalized racial segregation in the United States. But the Montgomery Bus Boycott of 1955–56 followed decades of organizing at both the national and local level. It was not even the first bus boycott. There had been one in Baton Rouge in 1953, and there had even been a protest against segregation on Montgomery trolley cars in 1900. What was different in Montgomery in 1955 was that local circumstances uniquely came together to allow the boycott to succeed, and then that success and the new civil rights infrastructure that emerged fueled additional protests across the Deep South, followed in 1964–65 by the voter registration efforts centered in Selma.

As for the Montgomery Bus Boycott, its essential facts have become so well known that they are now misleading. Every schoolchild knows that Rosa Parks got arrested and then Martin Luther King put an end to segregation and discrimination. Or, as Julian Bond put it: "Rosa sat down, Martin stood up, then the white folks saw the light and saved the day." In fact, Rosa Parks and Martin King may be the only civil rights figures today's typical schoolchild can identify. Even within Montgomery, mentioning the names of E. D. Nixon, Rufus Lewis, Ralph Abernathy, Fred Gray, Jo Ann Robinson, Solomon Seay Sr., Robert Graetz, Erna Dungee, or any of a host of other stalwarts of the boycott—for strategic reasons, they called it a "protest"—draws mostly blank stares.

Yet as the historian J. Mills Thornton III has convincingly shown, it was municipal circumstances and history in Montgomery, Birmingham, and Selma that gave rise to the quite distinctive civil rights showdowns in each city.

In Montgomery, the boycott was preceded by two decades of leadership by, among others, E. D. Nixon, who had served as president of local and state NAACP branches and was a protege of labor leader A. Philip Randolph, and Rufus Lewis, a former coach at Alabama State, the local black college, and a man so passionate about black citizenship that he devoted much of his life to organizing voter registration efforts. Jo Ann Robinson was another professor at Alabama State College and the president of the Women's Political Council, which had already tried at least once to start a boycott over mistreatment of black passengers on the city buses. Then in 1954, Martin Luther King Jr. arrived to become pastor of the most prestigious local black Baptist church, the same year that the 24-year-old Fred Gray passed the bar exam and opened his law office in Montgomery. The next year, President Eisenhower appointed the north Alabama Republican Frank M. Johnson Jr. as a U.S. District Judge in Montgomery, and the Lutheran Church sent Robert Graetz, a young white West Virginian, to pastor the all-black Trinity Lutheran Church that was practically next door to Raymond and Rosa Parks's apartment and just a block away from Nixon's home. There was also Clifford Durr, a white liberal attorney from a patrician family who had recently returned home from Washington after serving in the Roosevelt and Truman administrations; Durr's wife, Virginia, the sister-in-law of Supreme Court Justice Hugo Black, was a formidable woman who seemed to be friendly with every white racial liberal in the country, including Eleanor Roosevelt.

On the other side, but equally important to the success of

the boycott, you had a mayor, city attorney, prosecutor, and local judges who had joined or at least were in tacit agreement with the White Citizens' Councils—sometimes viewed, not incorrectly, as a white-collar KKK—that had sprung up across the South in the wake of *Brown*.

And then there was Rosa Parks. She was portrayed—for strategic and public relations reasons— by the boycott organizers and by her own words in the months following her arrest as a meek seamstress. In fact, Mrs. Parks was the secretary of the Montgomery NAACP, had lunch many days with attorney Gray discussing the bus situation and other vehicles of black mistreatment and humiliation, and the summer before her arrest had attended interracial workshops at the Highlander Folk School in Tennessee, a unique training center for labor, adult education, and race relations organizing. As Gray has described, she did not know that she would be arrested on December 1, but when the moment came, she was prepared.

Following her arrest, the local black leadership recognized immediately that they now had the perfect representative to challenge the city on the segregated bus seating and other injustices. The boycott was immediately put into place and a new organization, the Montgomery Improvement Association, was created to run it, with King elected as president.

At that early stage, the City of Montgomery might have killed the movement simply by agreeing to the modest initial demands put forth by the MIA: an end to rude treatment, implementation of the same seating policy as in effect in Mobile, Alabama, and the hiring of some black drivers for the bus routes in the black community. But the city attorney, Walter Knabe, and Jack Crenshaw, attorney for the bus company, no doubt fretting that the camel of integration would get his nose under the tent of segregation, rejected compromise in even the smallest form. The black community, meanwhile, had found itself surprisingly united in the boycott and gaining by the day more and more national attention and resources.

Thus Gray, with the behind-the-scenes counsel of both Durr and NAACP attorneys Robert Carter and Thurgood Marshall, decided to bypass city officials and attack segregation itself at the constitutional level. Locating as plaintiffs four other black women who had been arrested on Montgomery buses for the same violation as Parks (for fear of complicating her pending criminal appeal, Gray did not name her as a plaintiff in the civil case), he drew up a lawsuit and filed it in federal court, where it landed on the desk of District Judge Frank Johnson, who had been on the job for half a year.

Johnson saw the implications immediately. "Well, Syd," he later recalled telling his law clerk when the decision in *Browder v. Gayle* was about to be announced, "we're getting on this horse now. Let's ride it."

Because the case involved a direct conflict between local law and federal law—the new *Brown* doctrine—Johnson asked for the convening of a three-judge panel, which ruled 2–1 that Montgomery's ordinance requiring racially segregated bus seating was now illegal under the U.S. Constitution. City attorney Knabe, aided by Alabama Attorney General John Patterson, appealed. Because the decision came from a three-judge panel, it was a direct appeal to the U.S. Supreme Court, which affirmed the lower-court decision, without a hearing, in November 1956.

News of the decision reached Montgomery immediately, yet city officials remained obstinate. It took another few weeks for the final order to reach the federal court in Montgomery, and for federal marshals to serve a copy on Knabe and Mayor W. A. Gayle. Only then did the city announce that segregated seating would be ended, and the next morning, December 21, 1956, 382 days after it began, the Montgomery Bus Boycott concluded. Reverends King and Abernathy and Mrs. Parks were photographed boarding and riding on a city bus, sitting in the seats formerly reserved for whites.

In January 1957, a last spasm of white supremacist violence tormented the city. Several homes and churches were bombed. But the violence faded as whites grudgingly accepted the new order of things, and blacks returned to the buses, sitting where they wanted, even in the back if that was their preference.

Meanwhile, Rosa and Raymond Parks could no longer find jobs in Montgomery and moved to Detroit. Fred Gray stayed in Montgomery and began a remarkable series of lawsuits that knocked down segregation in schools, parks, housing, employment, and any other area where he could make a case.

King was now a national figure, and in the year after the boycott ended he joined with a half-dozen other ministers to form the Southern Christian Leadership Conference. This is the organization he moved to Atlanta in 1960 and then led in large-scale demonstrations in Albany in 1962, Birmingham in 1963, Selma in 1965, and Chicago in 1966. In these campaigns, just as in Montgomery, he used Christianity and the tactic of nonviolence to draw the support of not just blacks but whites and mainstream organizations like churches, unions, foundations, and, ultimately, the federal government and Congress.

Ralph Abernathy eventually followed his friend Martin to Atlanta, and succeeded him as SCLC president, but he remained in Montgomery longer than King. In 1961, his church—the black First Baptist Church; there is also a white First Baptist in Montgomery—became one of the scenes of a tense standoff between civil rights supporters and federal authorities on the one hand, and a KKK-led mob of white supremacists and state and local government on the other. The occasion was the 1961 Freedom Rides, an effort of CORE (the Congress of Racial Equality), with the support of the pacifist organization the Fellowship of Reconciliation. The interracial Riders boarded buses in Washington, D.C., for a planned journey to New Orleans with the goal of testing the new Kennedy administration's commitment to civil rights, specifically whether President John F. Kennedy and his attorney general brother, Robert, would enforce *Boynton v. Virginia*, a recent Supreme Court decision that barred segregation in bus terminal facilities. (Bruce Boynton, incidentally, was a Selma college student arrested in Richmond while on his way home from Howard University; today he is the Dallas County Attorney in Selma.)

Once again, Montgomery and buses would be linked over civil rights.

The Riders made it without much incident through Virginia, the Carolinas, and Georgia. But in Anniston, Alabama, one of their two buses was attacked by Klansmen and set on fire; the riders narrowly escaped death when an undercover officer who had been riding with them forced the mob back from the doors long enough to let the passengers escape. In Birmingham, the Riders on the second bus found a KKK mob waiting on them at the Trailways bus depot, with police mysteriously absent. The Riders were brutally beaten; at least one suffered permanent brain damage.

With the Freedom Ride in jeopardy, college students from Nashville, Tennessee, who had been active in that city's sit-ins the year before, arrived in Birmingham determined to carry on despite the admonishments of the Kennedys and King that to continue would be too dangerous. The young activists would not be deterred, and after a few days of negotiation, a deal was worked out between the administration and the Alabama governor, John Patterson, to provide state trooper escorts. A single bus then left Birmingham under state highway patrol protection on Saturday morning, May 20, 1961. At the Montgomery city limits, by pre-arrangement, the state patrol escort peeled away so the local police could take over. Unfortunately, as had happened in Birmingham, the local police were colluding with the KKK, and when the bus pulled into the

Greyhound terminal, there was a waiting mob of whites and just a few local police who did nothing to stop the ensuing attack on the Freedom Riders, accompanying news photographers, and even a personal representative of Attorney General Kennedy, John Siegenthaler, who was knocked unconscious.

The beatings and maimings that followed were even more brutal than those in Birmingham and people might well have been killed—the young Riders had all written their wills before setting out—had not the commander of the state highway patrol, Floyd Mann, learned of the local police perfidy and rushed to the scene, wading into the chaos with his revolver drawn. Two riders were already bloodied and unconscious on the ground but were still being beaten with pipes, baseball bats, and fists. Mann tried to get the attackers off them, then finally stood over the prostrate William Barbee, fired two shots into the air, and cried, "I'll shoot the next man who hits him. Stand back! There'll be no killing here today."

The battered Riders eventually received medical attention and went into hiding at local black homes. King, meanwhile, was notified of what had happened and rushed to Montgomery. A community rally was called for the next night, Sunday, at Abernathy's church. By the time some 1,500 local blacks, the Riders, news reporters, and one or two white supporters gathered inside the church, a second mob had formed outside. While King was on the phone inside the church pleading with Bobby Kennedy for help, the mob outside was becoming more menacing, throwing rocks through the church's stained glass windows and homemade incendiaries against the walls, and overturning and setting afire a car parked outside the church. President Kennedy had already dispatched several hundred federal marshals, who had formed a cordon around the church, but they were outnumbered 8 to 1 by the mob and were unable to control the scene. Tear gas intended to dispel the mob was instead blown back toward the marshals and drifted through the shattered windows into the church, choking the people trapped inside. Eventually Governor Patterson agreed to activate the National Guard, which soon arrived and put down the mob assault, after which the people inside the church were able to leave safely.

On a national level, the incident further tarnished Alabama's reputation and gained sympathy for the rightness of the civil rights cause. Interstate bus transportation was desegregated. Locally, the attack on the Freedom Riders resulted in a turning point in the official response to violence. Embarrassed by the events, Montgomery construction executive Winton Blount (a future U.S. Postmaster General) rallied local business leaders to denounce the mob action and pledge that it would not be allowed to happen again.

Birmingham, however, was a different story. When local activists led by the Reverend Fred Shuttlesworth (a co-founder of the SCLC) escalated protests in 1963 against discrimination in downtown department stores, the city responded with brutal tactics, including the use of attack dogs and high-pressure fire hoses to break up demonstrations. The SCLC had been asked to join in what became known as the Birmingham Campaign, and ultimately hundreds of demonstrators, including schoolchildren, were arrested. Both King and Abernathy were also arrested, and while imprisoned King penned his famous "Letter from Birmingham Jail" in response to local white clergy who decried the city's violent repression but argued that blacks were pushing too hard too quickly.

The dogs, fire hoses, club-wielding police, and mass arrests of children were vividly depicted in shocking photographs on the front pages of newspapers and in newscasts around the world, embarrassing the Kennedy administration and forcing it to take a more proactive stance on the side of civil rights and against Southern segregation laws and practices. Kennedy then proposed what eventually would become the Civil Rights Act of 1964. In September 1963—less than three weeks after a quarter of a million people had peaceably assembled in Washington and heard King's "I have a dream" speech—the Birmingham events reached a tragic climax when KKK members responded to a federal court order to integrate the city's public schools by setting off a dynamite bomb at the 16th Street Baptist Church. Klansmen killed the four girls who took the force of the blast, but Birmingham Police Commissioner "Bull" Connor and Alabama Governor George C. Wallace were blamed for creating the climate in which the white supremacist vigilantes felt emboldened to commit such crimes in defense of "the Southern way of life." This was the same Southern culture Wallace had trumpeted in his inaugural address, only nine months earlier, as "segregation now, segregation tomorrow, and segregation forever."

As in Montgomery, the violence caused moderate white leaders to pressure city officials for a change in tactics if not beliefs, and Birmingham began to desegregate. JFK was assassinated two months later, but his administration, the courts, Congress, and the public were clearly impacted by the intensifying civil rights movement, which was now challenging Jim Crow segregation with sit-ins, marches, demonstrations, rallies, and court actions throughout the Deep South.

In 1964, Kennedy's successor, Lyndon Johnson, himself a Southerner, signed the historic civil rights act that Kennedy had proposed, barring segregation in public accommodations. While some white-owned businesses held out as long as they could dodge the law by declaring that they were private clubs, and a few even closed rather than submit, many hotels, restaurants, stores, and other public venues desegregated immediately.

Meanwhile, the civil rights movement was increasingly shifting focus to voting rights. Beginning in 1963 in Selma and in adjacent heavily black counties, SNCC and SCLC leaders, a number of whom were subsequently beaten and/or jailed for their efforts, joined forces with local activists and ministers to educate the descendants of slaves about voting and to motivate them to endure the obstruction and vilification of local whites they would face when they attempted to get registered.

Demonstrations in early 1965 in Marion, Alabama, coincidentally the hometown of the wives of King, Abernathy, and SCLC lieutenant Andrew Young, led to the shooting death by a white state trooper of Jimmie Lee Jackson, a church deacon who had tried for four years to register in Perry County. Outrage over Jackson's death transferred to demonstrations in Selma, where Dallas County Sheriff Jim Clark was proving as effective a foil as Bull Connor had been in Birmingham, except that in Selma Clark was personally punching black ministers in the face and shoving black grandmothers to the ground. On Sunday, March 7, demonstrators had announced they would march the fifty miles from Selma to Montgomery, the state capital, to symbolically lay the death of Jackson at the feet of Governor Wallace.

As an orderly parade of some 600 marchers left downtown Selma and crossed over the Edmund Pettus Bridge across the Alabama River, they were confronted on the Montgomery side by a line of state troopers and sheriff's possemen, some mounted on horseback. As the demonstrators knelt to pray, the troopers and deputies fired tear gas and charged the demonstrators, clubbing, beating, and trampling them as they broke and ran back over the bridge seeking safety. This was all recorded by news media and predictably filled newspaper front pages and led nightly news broadcasts.

The initial march was led by SNCC Chairman John Lewis—then a young activist and veteran of the Freedom Rides and the sit-in movement and now a U.S. Congressman from Georgia—and SCLC lieutenant Hosea Williams. But the violence on what is now known as "Bloody Sunday" immediately brought to Selma not only King, Abernathy, and other SNCC and SCLC staff members, but also an unexpected and unprecedented flood of ministers, labor leaders, educators, public officials, and others from around the nation. One, the Reverend James Reeb of Boston, was beaten severely by KKK members on a downtown street and died of his injuries after being transported to a Birmingham hospital.

After two weeks of legal wrangling over the demonstrators' right to peacefully march and the state's obligation to protect them from vigilantes—including those wearing badges—a new start toward Montgomery was begun on March 21, culminating four days later in a demonstration of 25,000 persons at the steps of the Alabama capitol. King addressed the crowd and—through the news media, the nation—and gave one of his most powerful orations, declaring, "The end we seek is a society at peace with itself, a society that can live with its conscience . . . I know you are asking today, How long will it take? I come to say to you this afternoon, however difficult the moment, however frustrating the hour, it will not be long."

That night, Viola Liuzzo was martyred when a carload of KKK members spotted her driving, with a young black man beside her, along U.S. Highway 80 west of Montgomery after shuttling a load of marchers back to Selma. Liuzzo's shotgun-blast execution further shocked the nation and increased public support for passage of a voting rights bill. President Johnson had already spoken before Congress in support of such a bill. "What happened in Selma," Johnson said, "is part of a far larger movement which reaches into every section and state of America. It is the effort of American Negroes to secure for themselves the full blessings of American life. Their cause must be our cause, too, because it is not just Negroes but really it is all of us who must overcome the crippling legacy of bigotry and injustice." He closed with the refrain from what had become the civil rights anthem, "And we shall overcome." Martin Luther King Jr., watching on television, wept.

Johnson's bill passed as the Voting Rights Act of 1965, and the political landscape of Alabama and the entire nation did markedly change. Into the 1960s, some majority-black counties in rural Alabama and across the Deep South had not had a single black registered voter. Within a decade after the Voting Rights Act, some of the same counties had elected black sheriffs and probate judges. Within two decades, the percentage of black legislators in Alabama equaled the proportion of blacks in the state population. Schools, law enforcement, state and local governments, hospitals, most private businesses, and even some churches were desegregated.

Racism had by no means been defeated, but Jim Crow was dead. Many brave people struggled for civil rights all across the South, and Alabama had played a leading role. The sustained civil rights movements in Montgomery, Birmingham, and Selma, emerging from decades of local actions and from specific municipal circumstances, reflected the various types of civil rights actions that had also played out in towns and cities across the Deep South. Collectively, they made a movement that was rivaled only by the American Revolution and the American Civil War in significance in American history. And it happened in a not so indirect line from Jamestown to Selma.

About the Author

Horace Randall Williams is the editor-in-chief of NewSouth Books, which he co-founded with publisher Suzanne La Rosa in 2000. He is responsible for the editorial and production parts of NewSouth's publishing program. Since his first book in 1989, he has edited, published, and/or co-published more than 700 titles, which is believed to be more than any other general trade book editor and publisher in Alabama history. Under his own name, he's also the author, co-author, or editor of a dozen books. Before book publishing, he was a reporter, editor, and publisher for newspapers and magazines, and he worked a decade at the Southern Poverty Law Center, where he was the founding director of the Klanwatch Project. He is also the founder of the Capri Community Film Society, a graduate of Leadership Montgomery, and for more than two decades was a board member of the Montgomery Improvement Association, the organization originally created to coordinate the Montgomery Bus Boycott of 1955–56. He's a native of LaFayette, Alabama, a graduate of LaFayette High School and Samford University, and he lives in Montgomery, Alabama.

www.ingramcontent.com/pod-product-compliance
Lightning Source LLC
Chambersburg PA
CBHW021149020426
42331CB00005B/971